Three's A Crowd

These trios can be performed with any other combination of instruments within Book I.

Violin

A mix and match collection of 19 trio arrangements by James Power.

CHESTER MUSIC

London/New York/Paris/Sydney/Copenhagen/Berlin/Madrid/Tokyo

Contents

Exclusive distributors:
Chester Music
(A division of Music Sales Limited)
8/9 Frith Street, London W1D 3JB, England.

Music Sales Corporation
257 Park Avenue South, New York, NY 10010,
United States of America.

Music Sales Pty Limited
120 Rothschild Avenue, Rosebery, NSW 2018, Australia.

Order No. PM234106R
ISBN 0-7119-9374-2
This book © Copyright 2002 Chester Music
No part of this publication may be copied or reproduced in any form or by any
means including photocopying without prior permission from Chester Music.

The instruments featured on the cover are provided by
Macari's Musical Instruments, London.
Models provided by Truly Scrumptious and Norrie Carr.
Photography by George Taylor.
Cover design by Chloë Alexander.
Printed in the United Kingdom.

Swan Lake

Music by Peter Ilyich Tchaikovsky
(1840 - 1893)

3

Country Garden

Traditional Folk Dance

The Happy Farmer

Music by Robert Schumann
(1810 - 1856)

Minuet

Music by Ludwig Van Beethoven
(1770 - 1827)

Cutie Flootie

Music by James Power

to Coda ⊕

D

⊕ Coda

D.C.
al Coda

9

Morning Has Broken

Words by Eleanor Farjeon, Music Traditional

Irish Washerwoman

Irish Folk Song

Lincolnshire Poacher

Traditional

The Kerry Dance

Molloy/Traditional

When The Saints Go Marching In

Words by Katherine Purvis, Music by James Milton Black

17

The Wild Horseman

Music by Robert Schumann
(1810 - 1856)

18

Jingle Bells

Words & Music by J.S. Pierpont

God Rest Ye Merry, Gentlemen

Traditional

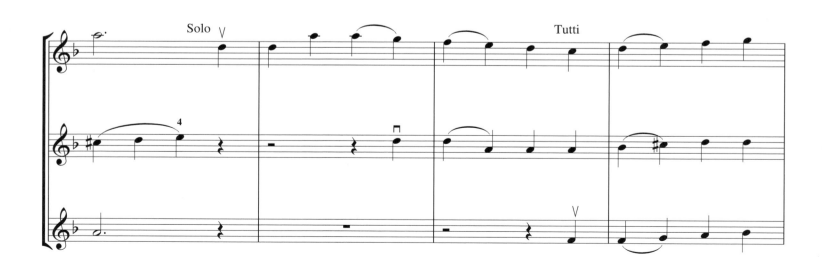

Sailors' Hornpipe

Traditional

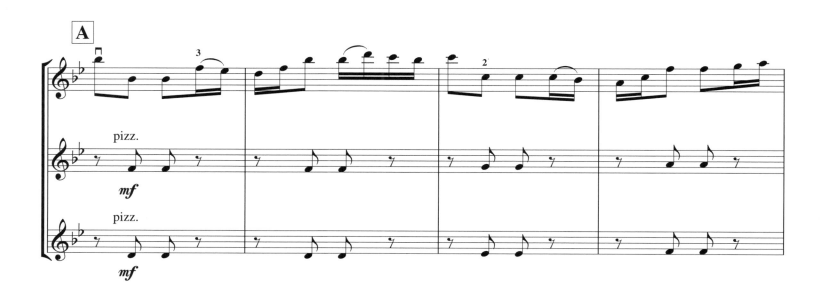

to Coda ⊕

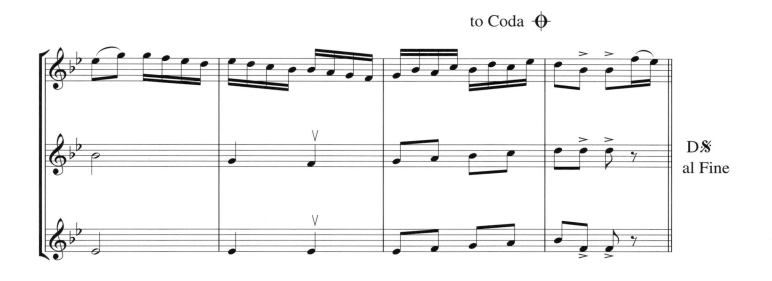

D.%
al Fine

⊕ Coda

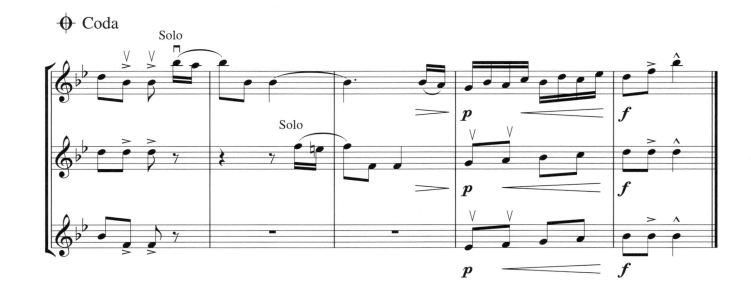

Mexican Hat Dance

Traditional

Giocoso   a tempo

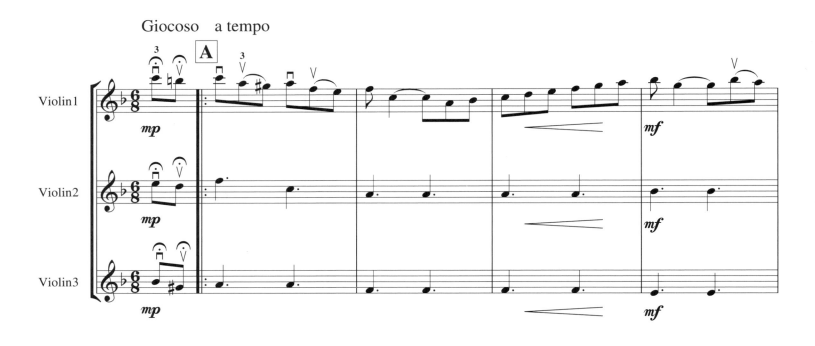

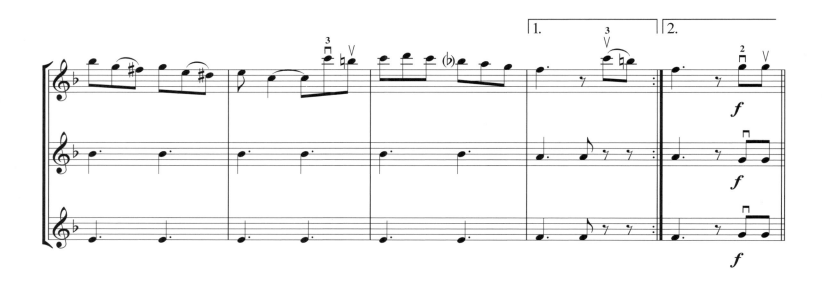

Phil The Fluter

Irish Traditional

Humoresque

Music by Dvořák
(1841 - 1904)

Fine

C

D.C.
al Fine

Allegro *from* Sonata in C major K545

Music by Wolfgang Amadeus Mozart
(1756 - 1791)

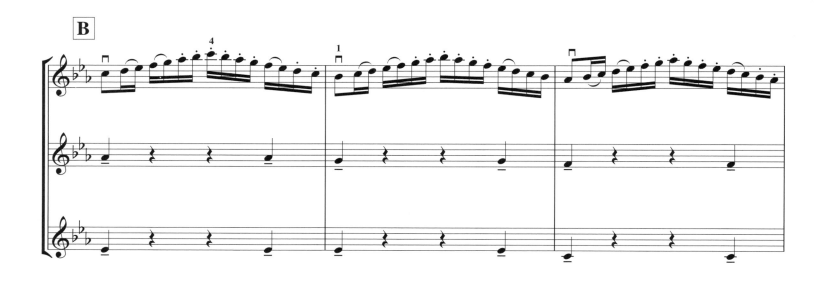

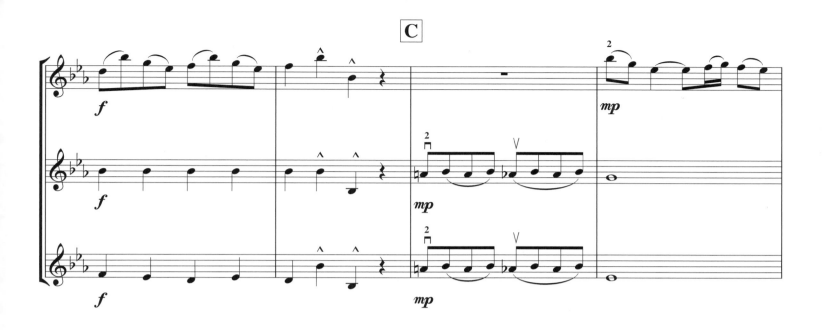

Scheherezade

Music by Rimsky-Korsakov
(1844 - 1908)